Published by Martori Enterprises II, Inc.
Vittorio Italiano, Pres.
Marlene Italiano, V. Pres.
Vizcaya Museum, Miami, Florida
Tel. 305 - 8568189
Copyright © 1983 Martori Enterprises II, Inc.
All photographs Copyright © 1983 Steven Brooke
First edition - July 1984
Printed in Italy

VIZCAYA

TEXT BY
DORIS BAYLEY LITTLEFIELD

PHOTOGRAPHS BY
STEVEN BROOKE

VIZCAYA MUSEUM AND GARDENS
3251 SOUTH MIAMI AVENUE
MIAMI, FLORIDA 33129

FOREWORD

Over two million people from near and far, high and low have been captivated by Vizcaya in the last third of a century. It is the unexpected and intense Italian adventure, in a beguilingly alien context that does it. It could, in fact, have been Vizcaya's fountains alone. Elinor Clark said of their antecedents in *Rome and a Villa*, "The very genius spent on them makes them shocking. They are not *objects d'art*, held off from life and treated with respect as they would be anywhere else; there is a closeness, and imminence of touch..."

Or more likely it was the total bedazzling experience, which she described in words which apply equally well to Vizcaya, "It is a deluge. You are a life way over your head, there is no getting out of it, except in the *beaux quartiers* which are not beaux at all but only pretentious; taste never functioned here on anything between the hovel and the grand palazzo."

VIZCAYA IS... where the dreamer is no more real than his dream, an historical monument, an anachronism, so much better that it has any right to be, an ambiance, a state of mind, the American dream, America's most beautiful palace, a great work of architecture. And it goes on – the most perfect melange, an exquisite expression of an age caught in amber, *deja vu* on a grand scale, an assemblage, and finally, glamorous of the Veneto, a stage set.

Let's just consider the last three for a momento. "Glamour", what an old-fashioned word! In my youth it was the highest compliment one could pay to a person, a place, an evening – or anything in general. When used at all now, it has a slightly tawdry ring. Words like people and places change character and meaning with time. But look it up and you will find that the only synonym is "magic". And that Vizcaya was, is, and always will be; the joint product of a unique and unlikely patron, James Deering, and three young geniuses, Hoffman the architect, Chalfin the interior designer, and Suarez of the gardens.

What an outlandish, outrageous scheme/dream to bring the essence of the Serene Republic of Venice to a small town on the shores of Biscayne Bay! But how miraculously they pulled it off. It wasn't a matter of the best that money could buy. More or less the same dollars were available for all the extravaganzas of Newport, Fifth Avenue and Bar Harbour, and Biltmore House, Whitehall, and San Simeon – you name it. The country is still dotted with the grand follies of the confused rich that were the talk of the town between the Civil War and the Great Depression. What set Vizcaya apart from its larger and smaller counterparts across our vast land was a rare fusion and superabundance of great good taste and sensitivity to nature, history, and all of the arts.

"Of the Veneto"? Vizcaya's creators at an early stage settled for "Spanish" as their logical style. But their imagination and open minds led them further and into the Veneto. This was the land of Andrea Palladio, the mid-16th century Italian architect, whose genius not only changed the face of his small but most blessed corner of our world, but also altered the history of architecture in Europe and eventually the United States, for centuries to come. His strong influence is still with us today though masked in new forms and materials.

Vizcaya is, in fact, more spiritually than specifically Palladian. It is elusive and often overlooked fact that Vizcaya's four facades are of more or less equal import architecturally, and the only obvious tribute is the central "Palladian window" on the second floor of the bay facade.

But the whole game was more subtle, ingenious and sensitive. They chose an infinitely more difficult, complex and sophisticated model and problem for themselves; and they conquered it! They wanted and created a house with a sense of time.

Their starting point was the Villa Rezzonico, a rather obscure great house of the Brenta River country – "The Brenta Riviera" – to which the Venetian aristocracy retreated whenever possible. As Contessa Volpi of the Villa Barbaro at Maser explained to guests there many years ago, "You must remember these houses were not meant to be lived in, they were only built for fun, to escape the summer heat of Venice or for a lark weekend when there was a new wine, or any other plausible excuse." Vizcaya followed that tradition, too. It was only really meant to function from Christmas to Easter.

Finally, "a stage set"? Vizcaya is pure theatre. Paul Chalfin would have been a superb-theatrical designer. Every room in Vizcaya is a *"set"*, the kind that used to cause a gasp of delight and spontaneous applause when the curtain went up on the first act the opening night of a new play. So ladies and gentlemen, you're on stage!

As always, either the Bible or Shakespeare provides our cue; in this case, the latter, in "As You Like It":

> *"All the world's a stage and all the men and women merely players;*
> *they have their exits and their entrances; and one man in his*
> *time plays many parts..."*

Carl J. Weinhardt, Jr.

INTRODUCTION

Vizcaya, now a museum of the European decorative arts, provides a unique experience for the visitor. To enjoy the Italian Renaissance-style villa and its superb gardens is to retreat into another world. The silence and shadow of the entrance drive through one of the few surviving sections of native South Florida hammock forest separates the estate from the noise and activity of the enlarging Miami metropolis.

Vizcaya was built in the years 1914 to 1916 as a winter home for the industrialist James Deering. Born November 12, 1859, in South Paris, Maine, James was the second son of William Deering, the developer of the Deering harvester machine. While James was still a boy, his father moved the family to Evanston, Illinois, where he built a factory for the production of farm machinery. James Deering was educated at Northwestern University and the Massachusetts Institute of Technology and entered the family business. In 1902 the firm merged with the McCormick Harvester Company and other companies to form the International Harvester Company. James Deering was a vice-president of the firm until 1919 when he resigned, and he continued to serve as a director to the time of his death in 1925. After his retirement from active business, he pursued his artistic and philanthropic interests and traveled extensively.

For many years Deering maintained a residence at Neuilly, outside of Paris, in addition to his Chicago home. He was decorated by the French government with the Legion of Honor for his contribution to the development of farm machinery. During his lifetime Deering made substantial contributions to charities and endowments, often anonymously. He suffered from pernicious anemia, a disease little understood at that time; and his doctors advised him to spend the winter months in a warm climate. Deering's parents had a winter home in Coconut Grove, Florida; and his older brother Charles had extensive property in Cutler, an area of southern Dade County. After considering other warm weather locations, James Deering decided to build in Miami, just south of the city limits. In 1912 he purchased a large tract of land from Mrs. William Brickell of the pioneer Miami family; and, with a subsequent purchase, his holdings comprised some 180 acres of shoreline, hammock and pineland. Deering asked Paul Chalfin, a young New York painter and designer, to advise him on his plans for a Florida house.

Paul Chalfin (1874-1959) attended Harvard College, trained as a painter at the New York Art Students' League and the École des Beaux Arts in Paris, and held for a short time the position of Curator of Asiatic Arts at the Boston Museum of Fine Arts. Leaving Boston in 1906, Chalfin studied and painted in France and Italy as the winner of the Lazarus Traveling Scholarship and was named a Fellow of the American Academy in Rome. On his return from Europe, he became associated with Elsie de Wolfe in her New York Studio of Interior Decoration; and it was through this connection that he met James Deering. Deering and Chalfin traveled to Europe to observe domestic architecture and to consider possible plans and purchases for the

Miami house. While the Spanish style of architecture had seemed the obvious choice because of Florida's Spanish heritage, it was the architecture of the country houses of the Italian Veneto that most interested the young designer and his patron.

James Deering was not an art collector in the manner of many other American millionaires; for, although he relied on Chalfin for advice, he reserved the right to have the final decision about major purchases. Together Deering and Chalfin made buying trips to Europe. There they selected the important architectural components for the proposed house – wall panels, ceilings, mantels, door cases, wrought iron grillwork, and the decorative elements – furniture, rugs, tapestries, sculpture and paintings. Chalfin scouted the New York dealers as well for many of the furnishings and accessories suitable for the house. James Deering took a great personal interest and pleasure in all matters pertaining to his home.

Paul Chalfin was not a trained architect, but he brought F. Burrall Hoffman into his association with James Deering for the architectural commission. Francis Burrall Hoffman, Jr. (1884-1980), a graduate of Harvard, received a diploma from the École des Beaux Arts in Paris where he studied architecture with Henri-Adolphe-Auguste Deglane. Hoffman began his career in the New York firm of Carrere and Hastings and in 1910 opened his own office in association with Harry Creighton Ingalls. After his accomplishments at Vizcaya, Hoffman conducted a distinguished career in New York and Paris. He designed many private homes and apartment buildings and at the age of ninety-eight was still working.

Hoffman began his drawings for the Deering house while visiting the site in 1913 and that year traveled to observe for himself the villas of Italy, for by this time Deering had decided that an Italian Mediterranean type of architecture would be suitable for his Florida house. Meanwhile the building site was being surveyed and prepared. Nothing of the size and scope of the proposed Vizcaya estate had been attempted in Florida before this time. Close to ten percent of the 1913 population of the young city of Miami, then about 10,500, were to work on the buildings and gardens.

James Deering's many purchases for the proposed house were stored and arranged in tentative room settings in the warehouse of P. W. French and Company in New York. Hoffman had to take into consideration the dimensions and proportions of these objects in planning the scale and configuration of the rooms for Vizcaya. There was little in building material that could be supplied locally. The native oolitic limestone was too friable for structural purposes but was used for lesser constructions, trim, garden decorations and rubble filling. Cuts of Florida quarry-keystone showing their inherent coral formations were used for steps and for many decorative elements. Quantities of Cuban limestone were imported for use where strength was needed. The structure of the house itself was to be reinforced bulk concrete with a stucco surface and stone trim. Handmade barrel tiles for the roof were obtained from existing buildings in Cuba.

It would have seemed logical to site the house on the natural limestone ridge above the tidal shoreline; but James Deering was very much concerned about the preservation of the native hammock growth existing in that area; and he decided that the house must be situated closer to Biscayne Bay. The necessary pilings and solid foundations constructed in this marshy ground cost Deering extra time and money but proved their value later when the house was exposed to the devastating force of the infamous hurricane of 1926. The gardens to be constructed south of the main house also required an extensive solid base to support their various levels and architectural elements.

In 1914 the young landscape architect Diego Suarez was commissioned to design the gardens. Born in Bogota, Colombia, Diego Suarez (1888-1974) was educated in Florence, Italy, as an architect. After his studies Suarez became interested in garden design and worked at the historic Villa La Pietra near Florence where the garden was being restored by the owner, Arthur Acton of the distinguished English family. James Deering and Paul Chalfin visited Acton, and Suarez was asked to show them several villas and gardens in the vicinity. This meeting with Deering led to the commission for Vizcaya's gardens. With the interruption of World War I, it took seven years for these gardens to be completed to Suarez' designs.

Suarez arranged Vizcaya's main garden in a fan-shaped plan with the central axis continuing the north-south axis of the house, leading the eye to a Baroque casino or garden house raised on an artificial hill or mount. Beyond the mount was a lagoon and the south garden, an area of tropically planted islands connected by decorative bridges. There, too, was a large boathouse with a roof garden and a small domed garden house called the Casba. These elements, as well as tennis courts, were connected with winding drives through groves of palms and other trees. The main gardens are based on Renaissance and Baroque designs inspired by Suarez' extensive knowledge of Italian gardens and their Roman antecedents in which there was a more conscious application of architectural design to the setting of the house. The various terraces and areas into which the garden scheme is divided are distinguished by walls, balustrades, sculpture, decorative urns as well as fountains, pools and cascades. Trimmed hedges and trees repeat the balanced architectural features, while French influence is seen in the elaborate curvilinear parterres.

To the west of the main residence, across the road that was to become South Miami Avenue, lay the farm section of the estate with buildings designed by Hoffman to resemble a small northern Italian village. Here lived the resident estate superintendent, chief engineer, boat captain, boat engineer, garage supervisor, poultry man and the fishing guide, as well as other key personnel. Along with garages and workshops, there were stables, a cow barn, a dairy and a poultry house. A pumphouse provided water for the extensive flower and vegetable gardens. There was a greenhouse and a large shadehouse for delicate plants. Pineapple, citrus and other fruit were grown. The estate could be nearly self-sufficient. Electricity for power and light came from Miami, and telephone service went to all parts of the estate through its own switchboard. The major buildings of the Farm Village remain today and will be restored to become a part of Vizcaya's museum complex.

James Deering named his estate Vizcaya, a Basque word translated as "an elevated place." The name brings to mind the maritime province of Vizcaya in northern Spain on the Bay of Biscay which is called the Gulf of Vizcaya by the Basques; Vizcaya being the old word for Biscay or Biscayne.

Deering wanted a handsome residence with every comfort and convenience, a winter home where he might entertain houseguests with boating, tennis, a swimming pool and pleasant gardens, although Vizcaya became more elaborate and more costly than he had at first envisioned. Deering's health was declining, but the pleasure he derived from planning and furnishing Vizcaya undoubtedly added a new and absorbing interest to his later years.

Deering and Chalfin had decided that Vizcaya would be designed and furnished to look as if it had stood on its site for some three hundred years with each generation of the resident family embellishing parts of the house in its own contemporary fashion. The whole represents four major styles: Renaissance, Baroque, Rococo and Neo-classic. The complexities of creating a harmonious architectural entity to house the wide variety of decorative elements purchased by Deering were ingeniously overcome by Burrall Hoffman. The structure creates the appearance of an Italian Renaissance villa. The rooms are arranged around a central courtyard with a ground floor loggia in the center of each of three sides and a main stairway in the fourth side, providing axial views to the bay and to the gardens. Two towers on the bayfront rise above the second floor roof line and contain guest bedrooms. The second floor consists of the owner's suite, the principal guest suite, additional guest bedrooms and an upstairs dining room or breakfast room, all opening onto galleries overlooking the central courtyard. The kitchens are on the second floor as well. In the towers on the west side of the house, an intermediate floor contains service and servants' rooms. The ground floor rooms are used for formal entertaining: the Reception Room, Renaissance Hall, Music Room, Tea Room, Banquet Hall and Mr. Deering's library. Below this floor is the basement with service and utility rooms; and on the north side of the house, where now the Museum has located a Gift Shop and Café with an outdoor terrace, were the billiard room, smoking room and bowling alley. There were dressing rooms for the swimming pool which extends from an interior decorated grotto out to the sunlit exterior. The house had every modern convenience: central heating, a vacuum cleaning system, a call system for the staff, many telephones, a fire sprinkler system, refrigeration by brine circulation, a dumbwaiter from the second floor kitchens and a service elevator as well as a passenger elevator.

The decoration of the interiors was the responsibility of Paul Chalfin, and his successful synthesis of furnishings and decorative elements that span some four hundred years in stylistic chronology testifies to his creative imagination. Chalfin achieved the effect of a home that is luxurious, beautifully appointed, yet intimate and comfortable. Each room conveys the general feeling of a period style with its historic furnishings to be used and enjoyed. [Although the Museum has had to make some changes in furniture arrangements to allow for the movement of the visitors through the house, the rooms are essentially as they were in Mr. Deering's day.]

While Paul Chalfin was the artistic supervisor for every phase of the planning and furnishing of the villa, he had the assistance of the finest artists and craftsmen.

Some of the more notable artists were: A. Stirling Calder (1870-1945), renowned sculptor, was responsible for the figures and decorations on the great Stone Barge; Gaston Lachaise (1882-1935), the designer of the stone peacocks for the Peacock Bridge leading to the south gardens; Robert Chanler (1872-1930), painter and designer, fashioned the marine grotto of the swimming pool with its underwater effects; Charles Cary Rumsey (1879-1922), sculptor, created the lead lizards and frogs decorating the fountain basin on the south terrace; Ettore Pellagatta (1881-1966), sculptor of many of the figures of native limestone that embellish the garden architecture; Paul Thevenez (1891-1921), Swiss painter, restored and completed the ceiling painting of the Casino loggia; Samuel Yellin (1885-1940), a master craftsman and designer in wrought iron whose work at Vizcaya included gates, grills and minor pieces for both house and gardens.

The main house with its seventy rooms required a staff of thirty during the winters of James Deering's residency. The owner occupied the house for about four months of each winter season beginning at Christmas in 1916. He frequently had family visitors and other houseguests and added local friends with their guests for luncheon parties. Deering's eighty-foot yacht NEPENTHE was often used for entertaining; he could comfortably accomodate twelve for luncheon. He enjoyed fishing on his forty-five-foot launch PSYCHE, and this boat could seat ten guests for a meal.

James Deering died September 21, 1925, on the S. S. PARIS, returning from France. Deering had never married; and Vizcaya was left to his heirs, daughters of his brother Charles. The estate, with a reduced staff to service it, was used infrequently by the family after Deering's death. About twenty years later, the family sold a section of the cultivated land south of the Farm Village for residential development and the south garden area on the bay for a school and hospital complex. The house and some twenty-eight acres of surrounding land were retained by the family in the hope that Vizcaya might become a cultural asset for the people of Miami. In 1952 Dade County purchased the land and buildings for one million dollars in revenue bonds (now paid) for the purpose of establishing an art museum. The furnishings and works of art were a donation from the heirs.

Today Vizcaya is a widely recognized museum of the European decorative arts operating on a self-sustaining basis and attracting some quarter of a million visitors annually.

Doris Bayley Littlefield
Curator of Collections
Vizcaya Museum and Gardens
Miami, Florida

JAMES DEERING
1859-1925

A watercolor portrait painted in 1917 by John Singer Sargent (1859-1925).

Black and white photographs courtesy of Vizcaya Museum Archives

Paul Chalfin,
Deering's artistic
supervisor for Vizcaya,
in a pastel portrait
by Albert Sterner in 1915.

John Singer Sargent, a
friend of James Deering's
brother Charles, painted
a series of watercolors
of Vizcaya in 1917.
This shows Sargent's
view of the South Arcade.

1

2

3

4

5

6

1 – *Construction of the house in February, 1915, as seen from Biscayne Bay.*

2 – *Construction of the house in April, 1915, as seen from the south.*

3 – *Construction of the house in July, 1915, the west facade is shown.*

4 – *In this early photograph of the garden construction, the foundations for the Mount and the Casino can be seen in the background.*

5 – *The south garden area during its construction. The small, domed Casba can be seen.*

6 – *The Mount and Casino construction nearing completion; the native limestone blocks, in their unfinished state, are ready for the sculptors. The grotto entrances, to left and right, will be embellished by carved figures of giants supporting the openings.*

An early aerial view of Vizcaya and its grounds.

Ground Floor Plan.

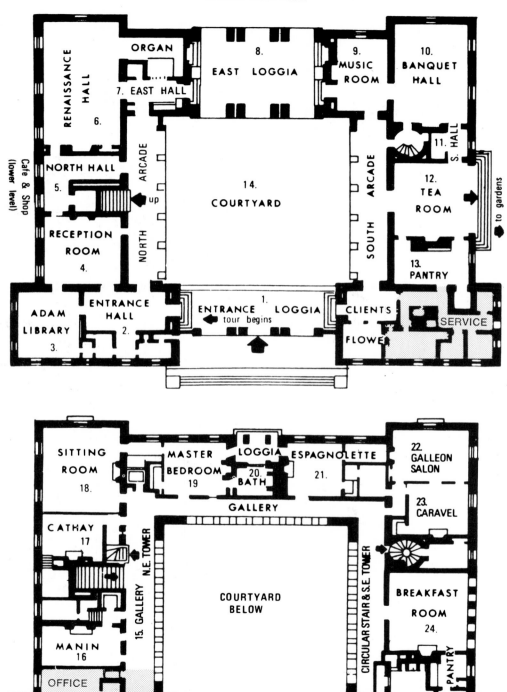

Ground Floor Plan:

- RENAISSANCE HALL 6.
- ORGAN
- 7. EAST HALL
- 8. EAST LOGGIA
- 9. MUSIC ROOM
- 10. BANQUET HALL
- NORTH HALL
- 5.
- NORTH ARCADE
- 14. COURTYARD
- up
- SOUTH ARCADE
- S. HALL
- 11.
- 12. TEA ROOM
- to gardens
- RECEPTION ROOM 4.
- Cafe & Shop (lower level)
- 13. PANTRY
- ADAM LIBRARY 3.
- ENTRANCE HALL 2.
- 1. ENTRANCE LOGGIA
- tour begins
- CLIENTS
- FLOWER
- SERVICE

Second Floor Plan.

- SITTING ROOM 18.
- MASTER BEDROOM 19
- LOGGIA
- 20. BATH
- ESPAGNOLETTE 21.
- 22. GALLEON SALON
- GALLERY
- 23. CARAVEL
- CATHAY 17
- 15. GALLERY
- N.E. TOWER
- COURTYARD BELOW
- CIRCULAR STAIR & S.E. TOWER
- BREAKFAST ROOM 24.
- MANIN 16
- OFFICE
- PANTRY
- STAFF
- SERVICE PASSAGE
- 26. LECTURE ROOM
- 25. KITCHEN

Second Floor Plan.

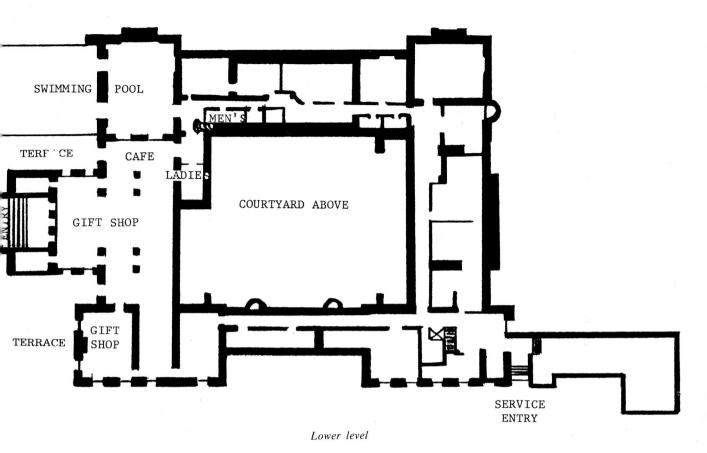

SWIMMING POOL

TERRACE   CAFE

MEN'S

LADIES

GIFT SHOP

COURTYARD ABOVE

ENTRY

TERRACE   GIFT SHOP

SERVICE ENTRY

Lower level

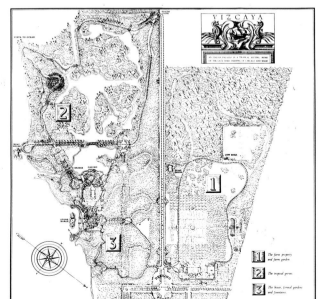

A schematic drawing of the Vizcaya estate.

1

2

3

4

5

1 –   *The main entrance gate to Vizcaya.*

2 –   *A sun-dappled glade is seen from the entrance drive.*

3, 4, 5 –   *The circular entrance plaza is accented by pairs of large sculptured terms, each surmounted by a decorative stone urn.*

19

6

6 – *The entrance drive, as it approaches the house, is paralleled by sculptured stone water courses with shell-shaped fountain basins, recalling those designed by Giacomo Vignola (1507-1573), for the Villa Lante near Viterbo. The oval forecourt has a central reflecting pool. The west, or entrance facade of the house shows an open loggia between the flanking towers.*

7 – *On either side of the forecourt stand imposing gateways of pink marble and Istrian stone brought from the Palazzo Bevilacqua-Lamassa at Verona. They are surmounted by sculptured seahorses of native limestone, one of James Deering's symbols for Vizcaya.*

8 – *A skillful blending of elements in the vaulted Entrance Loggia sets the tone for what is to come. Opposite the entrance gate is a fountain composition that might have been assembled by an Italian connoisseur in the period of the Renaissance. A statue of Bacchus, restored in the 17th-century, is flanked by sculptured putti astride sea monsters. Jets of water fall into a marble sarcophagus-shaped basin that dates from the time of the early Roman Empire. On either side are nobly proportioned urns of Egyptian granite placed on marble pedestals. The intricate pattern of the marble floor suggests a three-dimensional effect.*

9 – *The Neo-classic decoration of the Entrance Hall, with its geometrically patterned marble floor echoing the coffered ceiling, features French wallpaper panels printed from wood blocks made at the workshop of Joseph Dufour about 1814. Adjoining coat rooms are in the mid-18th-century style.*

8

10

11

10 – *The molded wall and ceiling decoration of the Library are derived from design* *by Robert Adam (1728-1792). The painting of the children of the Hon. Edward Go...* *ding is dated 1787 and signed by Richard Livesay (English, 1760-1823). the mahoga...* *center table is French, as is the 18th-century desk with painted panels. The carpet* *Spanish of Savonnerie type. Through the open door the Entrance Hall can be see...*

11 – *The seahorse, a symbol used throughout the Villa, forms a bookend on Mr. De* *ring's library desk.*

12 – *The Library fireplace features an Adam-style mantel of carved wood. Above is* *mid-19th-century Italian mosaic based on a Roman prototype.*

12

13 -

14

13 - The molded and painted plaster ceiling in the Reception Room was created i
the 18th-century for the Palazzo Rossi in Venice. The intricately carved, painted an
gilded boiserie is typical of the Piemonte and is complemented by the wall covering, a
exact reproduction by Franco Scalamandré of the original 18th-century wall silk wit
its delightful palm tree motif. The room is lighted by an 18th-century Venetian chande
lier and is furnished with French furniture of the Louis XV period. On the center tabl
are Chelsea figures of the Continents (1745-1750), and on the 18th-century Frenc
mantel is a bust by Louis Simon Boizot (1743-1809), of the Comtesse de Montbriar
The needlework rug is Portuguese work of the mid-18th-century.

14 - A small French table of the Louis XV period has a marquetry design of a musi
cal trophy and a tambour door of leather book backs.

15 - This view of the Reception Room shows an 18th-century French clock set in a
Italian tole bracket case on the mirror panel of the boiserie. The wall sconces are c
iron fashioned into vines supporting Meissen flowers and figurines. The Italian consol
table of the period displays armorial designs of the Aldobrandini family in its carve
detail and holds an Italian soft-paste porcelain group.

15

16

17

18

19

20

21

22

16 – Vermiculated carving in limestone adds architectural interest to the North Hall. The heavily carved 17th-century style door opens to the Renaissance Hall. On the right, in silhouette, is a replica of the Classical statue known as The Spinario or Thorn-puller.

17 – A private telephone room is decorated in the 18th-century Venetian manner.

18 – The mahogany entrance doors of the north facade feature interior bronze handles in the form of satyr heads.

19 – Columns of the Tea Room's south wall have seahorse-form drapery tie backs.

20 – Bronze figures of lizards on columns in the loggias are decorative tie backs for canvas awning panels.

21 – A Venetian gondola prow ornament in bronze is in the form of a hippocampus.

22 – This bronze figure of Silenus, companion of Bacchus, shows him as he is generally represented – an intoxicated, jovial, baldheaded old man.

23

24

25

30

26

23 – *The Renaissance Hall is a double-cube room with a beamed ceiling above a carved wood cornice which includes several original late 16th-century sections. In the room are three pairs of antique Roman columns of colored marble. The furniture is of 16th and 17th-century date; several pieces with historic family origins. The walnut trestle table is said to have belonged to the Farnese family of Naples. On it are a Spanish carved and gilded coffret of about 1500, a pair of wooden Gothic heraldic lions and two polychrome wooden figures bearing the Bontempi family name which were made in Umbria in the mid-16th century. Woven into the fine Hispano-Moresque carpet are the armorial bearings of the hereditary admiral of Castile, Fadrique Enriquez (d. 1473), and his wife, Marina de Ayala. At the end of the room can be seen two wall cases constructed for this setting from sections of 16th-century carved and gilded Spanish woodwork. The large escutcheon over the door on the right bears the arms of the Carmenotti family.*

24 – *Dominating the west wall of the Renaissance Hall is a massive 16th-century Caen stone fireplace originally from a French location. Flanking the fireplace are Renaissance doorways surmounted by 17th-century Italian marble busts.*

25 – *This detail of the Farnese table shows the heraldic winged sea-unicorns which retain traces of their original gilding.*

26 – *James Deering wanted a pipe organ; and this Welte-Mignon instrument, which can be played manually and electrically, was installed when the house was built. Paul Chalfin created a reredos effect incorporating baroque columns and entablature framing a 17th-century Neapolitan painting of the Holy Family.*

27

28

27, 28 – *The East Loggia opens to the terrace overlooking Biscayne Bay. The ceiling decoration features reliefs showing Apollo and the Nine Muses; and the floor is dramatically patterned in colored marbles. The late 18th-century pine doors, with sculptured bronze decoration and carved marble surrounds, came from a palazzo of the Torlonia family of Rome. The Torlonia arms appear at the top of the frame and are surmounted by 17th-century Italian marble busts. The early 20th-century scale model of Ponce de Leon's caravel, San Cristobal, suspended from the ceiling, is again a symbol of Vizcaya. In Mr. Deering's day the room was called the Open Loggia and, furnished with comfortable wicker furniture, made a pleasant place to enjoy the view of Biscayne Bay.*

29 – *The Music Room is decorated in the vivacious spirit of the Italian Rococo style. The canvas paneled walls and ceiling, painted in Milan in the mid-18th century, are decorated with shells, coral and curious marine forms. The early harpsichord, in an 18th-century case, is signed GIOVANNI BATTISTA BONI, CORTONA, 1619. The painted harp is French of the Louis XVI period. The 18th-century Venetian chandelier combines gilt metal foliage with glass flowers. Sections of a larger Aubusson carpet have been pieced together for the small room. The intimate scale of the room and its furniture is suited to the music of Mozart and Bach, first heard in a room such as this.*

30

31

30 – *The Banquet Hall evokes the Italian Renaissance. The ceiling is based o 16th-century ceiling in the Palazzo Gonzaga in Mantua. Below it hangs a 17th-cent velvet valance with gold-thread embroidery. There are three 16th-century tapestrie the room. The Flemish mille-fleur on the end wall was woven at Tournai. The Ferr tapestries on the wall at the right depict mythological scenes and once belonged to poet Robert Browning. Antique columns of brocatel marble flank a 15th-century f place carved of Tuscan "pietra serena". The early Italian Baroque doors of carved gilded wood came from a church sacristy. On the mantel is a portrait bust of a Ve tian senator dated about 1500. The northern Italian walnut refectory table of the n 16th century and the 17th-century Italian chairs are ornamented with intarsia dece tion. The late 15th-century Italian sacristy cupboard at the right serves as a sidebo On the marble and terrazzo floor is a colorfully embroidered 17th-century Po guese rug.*

31 – *The sacristy cupboard with intarsia panels displays part of a collection of lian Renaissance bronze mortars and a 15th-century Flemish brass alms plate*

32 – *The marble table-supports in the form of winged lion-griffins are particul fine examples of Roman decorative sculpture and date from the middle of the first tury A.D.*

3

33

34

36

35

33 – The enclosed loggia or Tea Room opens on the terraces and gardens with a wall of stained glass which displays the seahorse and caravel – decorative symbols seen throughout Vizcaya.

34 – The richly colored marble floor of the Tea Room and the 17th-century Nubian marble mantelpiece are exceptional. Neo-classic themes are seen in the modeled ceiling, cornice and frieze as well as in the horizontal panels painted with Roman-inspired grotesques.

35 – The large canvas panels are extravagant and imaginative scenes of fantastic Classical cityscapes as painted by Neapolitan scenery painters of the late 18th century. A replica of the Dancing Faun, a statue found in the ruins of Pompeii, is placed on an Empire pedestal.

36 – Seen at night, the Tea Room presents the illusion of an imaginative stage setting.

37

38

39

37 – *The vaulted South Arcade appears today as it did when Sargent painted it in 1917. The flooring combines old Cuban tiles with cuts of Florida quarry-keystone revealing the patterns of coral growth. To the right is the imposing gateway to the Tea Room. The bronze and iron gates set in an arch of red Verona marble came from a palazzo of the Pisani family in Venice.*

38 – *The characteristic features of the Italian Renaissance-styled architecture can be seen in the open Courtyard planted with a variety of tropical vegetation. On the left is the main stairway ascending to the galleried second floor.*

39 – *From the Gallery the Courtyard is seen as a pleasant place for informal entertaining. The 17th-century dolphin fountain is flanked by antique Roman columns supporting a wrought iron framework featuring the caravel symbol made by Samuel Yellin (1885-1940).*

40

41

40 – *The second floor rooms open to the Galleries. The flooring is old Cuban tile, and cypress beams support the roof. To the left is the main stairway and beyond is the stairway to the north tower guest rooms. At the end of this Gallery is the passenger elevator.*

41 – *The main stairway rises in a vaulted passage. On the landing is a 17th-century marble statue of Pan in an arched niche.*

42 – *The landing of the main stairway closes with an ornamental wrought iron gate of 17th-century date which is set in a matching framework made by Samuel Yellin.*

42

43

44

45

46

43 – *Vizcaya's guest rooms were given names often suggestive of their decorative period. Manin bedroom is thus named for Daniele Manin (1804-1857), president of the 1848 Venetian republic formed to check the Austrian domination of Venice. Manin is furnished in the style of Biedermeier, a provincial version of the Empire style especially popular in Germany and Austria from about 1820 to 1860. The set of Biedermeier secretary-desk, bed and small cabinet is made of curly sycamore wood with inlay and steel trim.*

45 – *The Otis elevator car has been decorated in a style suitable to the luxury of the house.*

44 – *A north tower bedroom named Lady Hamilton displays a bed made in Naples about 1790. Fashioned in the Neo-classic style popular at that time, it has a silk gold-embroidered headboard. The bed is said to have belonged to Emma, the wife of Sir William Hamilton, British envoy to the court of Naples. Emma is perhaps better known as the mistress of Admiral Horatio Nelson.*

46 – *Chinoiserie, a decorative style using Chinese themes as interpreted by 18th-century European artists, sets the whimsical mood of the Cathay bedroom. The furniture is largely Italian. Chinese ornaments, wall silks and rug complete the room.*

47

48

47 – James Deering's second floor sitting room is Neo-classical in feeling and furnishings. The Italian woodwork of the late 18th century is complemented by panels of French silk of the Louis XVI period. The adjoining desks are of the French Empire period. The round marble-topped table is signed Claude Chapuis (w. 1797-1818). The design of the Savonnerie carpet incorporates the symbols of the zodiac.

48 – In this view the ceiling decoration can be seen; incorporating the seahorse symbol of Vizcaya, it was designed by Paul Chalfin. The round marble-topped table seen here at the end of the room is an Italian Empire-style piece. On the large modern mahogany table against the wall is a terra-cotta figure group by Albert Carrier Belleuse (1824-1887).

49 – The carved marble mantel was designed by Robert Adam for Rathfarnham Castle in Dublin. It is flanked by carved, painted and gilded wooden columns perhaps made by Giuseppe Bonzanigo (1745-1820), who worked near Turin, Italy.

50 – The small French drop-side sofa of mahogany is one of two in the room of the Neo-classic period. Called a méridienne, it is similar in design to those painted on ancient Greek vases.

50

51

52

53

51 – James Deering's bedroom is decorated with elements of the Neo-classic style. The French Empire period mahogany furniture is highlighted by elaborate gilt-bronze mounts. Silk covers the walls, and the carpet is an 18th-century Aubusson.

52 – In the bedroom the 1790 Irish fireplace is again a Robert Adam style here with Neo-classical motifs in colored inlay by Bossi. The small Louis XVI table has a silk-embroidered landscape panel set into its top surface. Through the doorway can be seen the elaborate master bathroom.

53 – The Neo-classical detail of the cornice and frieze is accented with representations of the moon's faces done in gold leaf.

54 – While each guest bedroom at Vizcaya has its own well-appointed bathroom, Deering's own bath is the most elaborate. An embroidered linen ceiling canopy suggests a Napoleonic campaign tent. Marble walls are decorated with Sheffield silver plaques. Gold-plated faucets control the flow of fresh or sea water. A custom-designed shaving stand, piped for water, is placed in front of doors that open to a balcony overlooking Biscayne Bay.

54

55

56

55 – Espagnolette bedroom is decorated and furnished with a feeling of 18th-century opulence. Rococo curvilinear designs form the decorative plaster cove and frame the canvas wall panels painted with scenes recalling the work of Watteau. The painted furniture is a Venetian interpretation of the French Rococo style, of which the elegantly decorated bed is an outstanding example. A silk Tabriz rug complements the room.

56 – Above the 18th-century Italian fireplace of grey marble is an overmantel arrangement composed by Chalfin of an Italian mirror overlaid with carved and gilded wood and girandoles fashioned from 18th-century Venetian vases. The chairs and small table are of the period.

57 – Paul Chalfin chose the names of sailing vessels for the rooms of Vizcaya's principal guest suite, the salon called Galleon and the adjoining bedroom, Caravel. In Galleon, pictured here, the wall panels are marbleized in 18th-century Venetian style and inset with Italian landscape paintings in the manner of Francesco Zuccarelli (1702-1788). Italian portraits of the period flank the English mantel of carved wood. At the right is one of a pair of painted Venetian wardrobes. The mid-18th-century Italian desk is of tulipwood. The English commode of the same period is rosewood with marquetry ornamentation. The 18th-century carpet is of the Savonnerie type.

58

58 – *The roof of the house as seen from a tower window has its own architectonic elements. The seahorse emblem can be seen on the weather vane.*

59 – *This cantilevered stairway displays a spiral pattern.*

60 – *Goyesca bedroom, in the south tower, is decorated and furnished in the Neo-classic style. The painted canvas wall panels, with Roman-inspired grotesque decoration, are part of the set used in the Tea Room. Details of the bed canopy repeat the wall motifs.*

59

60

61 – Ch'ien Lung Foo dogs guard the entrance to the second floor dining room called the Breakfast Room. A 16th-century Italian arch of carved stone frames the view beyond.

62 – Glass doors are designed to slide back into the wall, leaving the garden side of the room completely open as for a loggia and presenting a broad view of the main gardens.

63

64

63 – *The Breakfast Room is lined with 18th-century marine murals in the man[...] of Claude Joseph Vernet (French, 1714-1789). Chinoiserie elements include the c[...] ved wood chimney piece and a pair of large 18th-century French terra-cotta figur[...] The chairs, finished in ted lacquer and gilt, are 18th-century Venetian. To the ri[...] can be seen an eight-fold Coromandel screen.*

64 – *One of two Imperial Ming porcelain bowls of the Chia Ch'ing period (15[...] 1566).*

– *The gardens, viewed from the Breakfast Room, show the fan-shaped plan with its balanced architec-*
ral features, water displays and traditional Italian use of greenery in shaped grass plots, clipped hedges
d trimmed trees. The curvilinear designs of the parterres show a French influence. These European-style
ntings are created with tropical vegetation.

66

67

68

69

66 – *The small room for arranging flowers has gaily painted door panels and wall cupboards in an 18th-century Venetian style.*

67 – *A muscular arm forms a 17th-century Venetian lighting fixture.*

68 – *The galleries and arcades are furnished with period pieces. This painted cassapanca is flanked by large pottery storage jars. That on the right carries the heraldic device of the Scaliger family of Verona.*

69 – *A bronze basin showing the forms of water buffalo is by the 20th-century Roman sculptor Duilio Cambellotti.*

70

71

72

70 – *This pantry cupboard displays examples of the Quimper ware used for informal meals in James Deering's day. Quimper faience has been made in Brittany from 1690 to the present.*

71 – *Deering's eightly-foot yacht NEPENTHE and his forty-five-foot launch PSYCHE were fitted with special appointments. English Cauldon bone china with sterling silver rims displays each boat's name with Deering's own yacht burgee and the pennant of the New York Yacht Club.*

72 – *The main kitchens, located on the second floor, had facilities for preparing meals for a large number of guests. The range incorporates cooking units for coal, gas and charcoal broiling.*

73

74

75

–   The east front of the villa, overlooking Biscayne Bay, is seen from the boat landing. This facade, ~~th~~ its tall corner towers, recalls the Renaissance fortress-like appearance of its prototype, the Villa Rez-~~ni~~co at Bassano del Grappa in the Italian Veneto; but here the central portion lightens the effect. The ~~at~~ Stone Barge at the left acts as a breakwater.

–   The pediment of the east facade is surmounted by the seahorse emblem on a weathervane and dis-~~ay~~s a sundial with the Latin inscription that translates: "Accept the gifts of the present hour joyfully and ~~i~~nquish them stoically."

–   The great Stone Barge, which acts as a breakwater at the bayfont of the house, displays sculpture ~~si~~gned by A. Stirling Calder (1870-1945) as "the delights and terrors of the sea."

–   At one end of the sea wall promenade, a delightful Tea House of French inspiration offers a cool ~~retreat~~ at the water's edge.

77

78

77 – The south facade of the villa is seen from the parterre of the main ga_
den. The ground floor loggia is the Tea Room and above is the Breakfast Roo_
with its sliding doors open to the air.

78 – There are many 17th and 18th-century decorative urns as gard_
accents.

79 – Lead frogs and lizards by Charles Cary Rumsey (1879-1922) decora_
the sarcophagus-shaped fountain basin on the south terrace.

79

80

80 – *The central axis of the garden, seen from the house, is defined by the island pool and the water stairway leading to the Casino on the Mount.*

81 – *An 18th-century Venetian statue personifies Virtue.*

81

82

83

82, 83 – *The cross axis of the garden is defined by the balanced placement of semi-circular pools and pairs of vine-clad domed gazebos.*

84

85

84, 85 –   *Marble columns supporting 18th-century Italian busts of Carrara marble and 17th-century urns from Messina ring the semi-circular garden pool with its interesting wrought iron railing designed by Samuel Yellin.*

86

87

86, 88 – *Dramatic giants, carved of native limestone, support the entrance each of the shell lined grottos that flank the water stairway leading to Mount. Inside the grottos there are stone benches; and a fountain drips of water.*

87 – *Varying surface treatments enliven the walls of the Mount which decorated with 18th-century Carrara marble busts.*

89 –   *Water from a jet in the marble font falls into a circular basin and then drops to the lowest level through a series of basins. This water stairway is reminiscent of that at the Villa Corsini in Rome.*

90 –   *The Casino, a house in miniature, provides a destination for a walk in the gardens. The small interior rooms, decorated in 18th-century style, are furnished for serving tea or sitting by a wood fire. The airy, open loggia offers a view towards the waterway beyond.*

91

92

93

91 – *The ceiling of the Casino loggia combines fresco from the 18th-century school of Tiepolo with additions by the Swiss painter Paul Thevenez (1891-1921).*

92 – *Adorned heads carved in white marble surmount a cipollino marble pedestal.*

93 – *An 18th-century stone sculpture of a dwarf, of the kind often seen in Italian gardens, stands on the wall of the Mount.*

94 – *The south or waterway facade of the Casino. On the ground level arches open to a sculptured stone grotto. Stairways at each side rise in Baroque curves to the level above.*

95

95 –   *On each side of the Mount, there are broad flights of steps, here leading to the Fountain Garden. Tracks are built on the steps in Italian fashion for the gardeners' wheeled carts.*

96 –   *The central axis of the garden is seen from the elevation of the Mount. In the foreground water jets from a 16th-century marble font.*

96

97

98

99

100

101

97 – *Along the east and west terrace walks, there are 17th and 18th-century statues of mythological gods and goddesses and allegorical figures.*

98 – *Winter is personified by an old man wrapping his cloak around him.*

99 – *A statue of Minerva, Roman goddess of wisdom and the arts.*

100 – *Neptune, god of the sea, with a dolphin.*

101 – *Apollo, Greek and Roman god of poetry and music, is shown with his lyre.*

102

102 – *Standing on the ornamental bridge over the waterway which once divided the formal gardens frothe south garden area, you look towards the Fountain Garden with its pattern of water channels and i
central structure which once stood in the town square of Bassano di Sutri. In the foreground are peacoc
topped columns and a tropical fish pool with sea shell decoration.*

103 – *A small 16th-century carved stone sarcophagus displays elements of Classical derivation as we
as many curious motifs.*

104 – *The Bassano di Sutri fountain, of travertine, shows many interesting details. It is in the style c
Jacopo Vignola (1507-1573), architect and sculptor.*

105 – *Gaston Lachaise (1882-1935) designed the stone peacocks surmounting twisted columns.*

104

105

106 – *From the elevation of the east terrace walk the intric⟨ designs of the parterre can be discerned.*

107 – *The greenery of the garden is seasonally enlivened by bright bougainvillea and begonias.*

108 – *Among the many marble urns salvaged from the ruins of a garden in Messina, Sicily, after the 1908 earthquake, several display curiously carved grotesque faces.*

108

109

110

111

112

109 – *This small garden in the form of a verdure theatre in the 18th-century style is similar to that at the Villa Gori near Siena. A marble balustrade forms the balcony: a parterre decorates the orchestra; a low wall elevates the stage with its wings of trimmed hedges.*

110 – *This small lead figure of Pulcinella brings to mind the Italian commedia dell'arte.*

111 – *English lead figures of a shepherd and shepherdess in the Theatre Garden.*

112 – *Rusticated native limestone frames the arched entrances to the Secret Garden. One of a number of curiously carved stone faces appears as an architectural decoration above the arch.*

113

113 – *In the Renaissance tradition a walled Secret Garden, inspired by that of the Villa Gamberaia near Florence, offers a private retreat from the formality of the house. Rusticated stonework accents the walls and forms wall-pockets for plants. The archway to the left leads to the bayfront. Steps at each side of the garden give access to a balustraded walk where one may look to the bay or turn to view the main garden.*

114 – *This elaborate composition is constructed of several 18th-century Italian elements. In the small grotto below the scallop-shell canopy there is a dripping fountain.*

115 – *The faces carved in the native limestone add interesting and often amusing details to the garden architecture.*
(next page - left)

116 – *The grotto entrance to the Secret Garden drips cool water among green ferns. Through its arch can be seen one of the domed gazebos.*
(next page - right)

11

117

117 – *The swimming pool extends to the sunlit exterior fr*
a wonderfully imaginative grotto beneath the house.

118, 119, 120 – *Here the swimmer sees an underwater fa*
tasy of marine life, corals and aquatic plants modeled on
vaulted ceiling by Robert Chanler (1872-1930). Sea shells a
carved stone decorate the walls with their dripping fountai
The floor is patterned in colored marbles.

8

119

120

121

121 – *Night brings an unforgettable feeling of enchantment*
Vizcaya's gardens.

EXCERPTS FROM

SOUND AND LIGHT AT VIZCAYA

Text: Herb Hiller
Editor: Carl Weinhardt
Narrator: Thomas Hoving

James Deering chose to be here over any place in the world. This was his winter home. If you knew Miami at the turn of the century when Mr. Deering first arrived here, you might wonder why. Until the railroad was pushed down through the swamps from Palm Beach in 1896, Miami was one of the most isolated spots in America.

He had already rejected Egypt, North Africa, the Riviera, Spain, South America, the South Seas, and the Orient – before deciding on Miami. He began building Vizcaya exactly 400 years after Ponce de Leon had sailed into the bay. It became James Deering's destiny, in a sliver of time, to complete the act of Ponce by implanting ashore the artistic legacy of the Renaissance. Think of it! But now it was 1913. The Balkan Wars began. In a year Europe would burst the world into raging conflict. It was the end of Edwardian civility, the last moment of what we now see as American Renaissance life.

The inspiration for Vizcaya chiefly came from four men. In addition to Mr. Deering, they were: F. Burrall Hoffman, Jr., architect "to the manner born," whose adaptation of Renaissance architecture to the Tropics was to launch a distinguished career that continued through 70 years into the 1980s; Paul Chalfin, a voluptuary and failed painter, who triumphed as the artistic genius of Vizcaya and later fell into bitternees and obscurity; and Diego Suarez, whose landscape artistry at Vizcaya tempered the tropical sun and raised up gardens unrivaled in all America.

Sixty years after starting work on the plans for Vizcaya, Hoffman recalled the beginning:

> It was like a story. As you try to write a story, you think of things that might fit into it. Then, finally you get a whole vision of how you want things to go. Maybe it started from something you've seen. Maybe it's something you just have in your mind. Then you try to do it.

Let's begin with the west view of the house that architect Hoffman designed. Its origins lay in the Veneto, the region surrounding Venice, one of the richest of Renaissance cities. There in the 15th and 16th centuries, the recently rediscovered principles of classical architecture were elaborated with new beauty in designs for dwellings of the ascendant princes of commerce.

The aristocracy of Venice began regular retreats, fleeing not from war, but to escape the pressures of commerce and to enjoy a new wine in the cool Alpine foothills. They sailed in a procession of luxurious, gilded barges along the Brenta River to their dazzling villas among the willows; places of perfect indulgence.

In a feat of extraordinary genius, Hoffman took the totally foreign world of Renaissance elements and amenably applied them to tropical surroundings. Hoffman would receive commissions from millionaires throughout his long career. But never, never would he or anyone else in America create such splendor in wilderness.

The north, or "Michelangelo" facade of the house, shows the impassiveness and great strength of 16th century Italian architecture. By contrast to the other facades the detailing is sparse and severe. That was part of the strategy, the "game." Chalfin explains in his own words:

> *I think I can say that Vizcaya is as much the result of a game which Mr. Deering and I worked out for ourselves as it was of studying and dreaming and working with an Italian palazzo decided upon.*

Each guest room or suite had its own romantic name selected by Chalfin to suit the decor – or sometimes merely his whim.

Chalfin turned out to be much more than an art advisor. He fulfilled on a dazzling scale James Deering's wish for a winter home. He dared to reproduce in art and design that spanned the centuries, a fantasy, gradually but ever so effectively coaxed from the wealth of a tiring millionaire. He transformed Mr. Deering's ambition for a modest country house in a warm climate to a legendary estate that marks the twilight of splendor.

In a way, Hoffman's challenge was more difficult. It was he who had to create the monumental theater to house Chalfin's settings according to the harmony of scale that was so dear to their patron. Hoffman's skill ultimately served to weave the entire inventory into some 50 rooms with a beguiling sense of effortlessness.

Mr. Deering might have surveyed the mighty seawall and boat landing where his graceful boats, *Psyche* and *Nepenthe*, frequently rode gently on their moorings. *Nepenthe*, at 80 feet, could accommodate 12 in comfort. She was elaborately appointed with china, crystal, and down to such refinements as engraved place cards and a player piano. The 45-foot *Psyche* could handle an overflow of guests up to 10.

On the other arm of the seawall rose the delicate latticed Tea House which Hoffman derived from a pavilion in the gardens of Versailles. Mr. Deering adored it. He often served guests drinks and late afternoon tea under its fanciful dome. As they sat on marble benches in the elegant retreat, visitors never failed to exclaim over the extraordinary breakwater for the small harbor. The idea is at least as old as Hadrian's artifice with an island in the Tiber. The form later became a symbol of St. Peter. Its use was theoretically restricted to families which had produced a Cardinal of the Church. What is it?

A great stone Barge!

To fully realize the genius of the Barge, imagine that it doesn't exist – and that the Villa stares out over a flat plane of water like any seaside house. Anchored forever, the magic ship creates a sense of middle distance. With its greenery and fountains, also breaks the daytime glare and finally creates the superb climax to that long promenade of the Entrance Plaza.

Mr. Deering had expected the house to be finished in 18 months. Instead, two years and seven months elapsed before he actually moved in on Christmas Day, 1916. The small çannon, now in the East Loggia, boomed the start of festivities over the bay. The guests and servants were in Italian costume. There was music. Food was served. And there was much excitement and rejoicing.

The long dream was realized!

John Singer Sargent spent part of the winter of 1917 here. While war raged in Europe he wrote of Vizcaya, "It combines Venice, Frascati and Aranjuez, and all that one is never likely to see again."

The garden is conceived as a vast room, walled in with terraces and backed by formal vegetation and forests. It terminates by the house and at the far end by the Mount and the Casino. The garden floor is elaborately patterned with low clipped hedges giving the effect of an oriental carpet. Parterres, as these patterns are called, date back to Roman times.

The main feature of the landscape is the Mount with its Water Stairway. The Mount is highlighted by the beautiful Casino with its two small rooms, decorated in the rococo style. It was not a casino as we know the word today, not meant to indulge just the passion for gambling. For Chalfin it meant unbridled indulgence in fantasy:

> *What was a Casino for? For one to dream in or perhaps to weep; for two to steal to; for three to sing and for eight to dance in. Or perhaps the footmen – just liveried boys from the farm – had fetched and displayed hampers of cold fowls and sherry and sorbets made from the strawberries that ripened – even in winter. A Casino held itself a household in miniature, was a playhouse for an hour, the great establishment with all its etiquette abbreviated and curtailed, but unbroken. For days perhaps it slept – dawn, noon, and night – awakening for its brief function, and then went to rest again to the sighs and gurglings of its fountains.*

By 1922 everything was pretty well finished. The gardens were actually astonishing. They were unrivaled in the Western world outside Europe. None touches the grandeur of scale at Versailles; those at the Villa d'Este are more spectacular; but no existing gardens of the formal type combine the elements of the Italian hill garden with those of tropical vegetation as do Vizcaya's. Including the farm and gardens, Vizcaya covered 180 acres.

James Deering enjoyed just eight winters at Vizcaya, only the last two with the gardens complete. That he luxuriated in his creation there is no doubt.

In a note to Paul Chalfin in 1922 he enclosed a photograph of the Casino taken from the lake to the south. The note read:

> *If proportion is the highest expression of beauty, as I believe it is, I do not know where you would go to find anything more beautiful than what is shown on the enclosed photograph.*

Such beauty and the life of leisurely refinement were passing. As James Deering's health failed, so did the world that sustained him. War and its aftermath had unleashed inflation, income taxes, labor disputes, and a mood of "live for the moment." Prohibition bred disrespect for the law. Population shifts snapped ties of sentiment and the dollar became almighty. Miami began to publicize itself with alligator wrestlers. Miami Beach was promoted with elephants. This was boom time! Real estate prices were rocketing, gambling was out in the open, and speakeasy living rampant. Pineapple plantations were uprooted for housing developments. Yet Vizcaya set the standard for Mediterrean architecture in South Florida that survives to our time. Nothing was done again on its scale, but modest approximations became the marks of many communities such as those promoted by George Merrick in Coral Gables and Addison Mizner in Palm Beach.

Then in 1925, James Deering, returning from France on the *S. S. Paris*, died.

So the story is told.

What is Vizcaya but *deja vu* on a grand scale? A stage set, real and unreal, a glamorous assemblage of what was once the American dream. It is a state of mind now an anachronism, an historical moment, the exquisite expression of an age caught in amber... so much better than it has any right to be. Vizcaya was a dream before it became a treasure. Let the dream remain a treasure with you...

VIZCAYA MUSEUM AND GARDENS
3251 SOUTH MIAMI AVENUE
MIAMI, FLORIDA 33129